Hold the Pickles

Vicki Grant

orca currents

ORCA BOOK PUBLISHERS

Library and Archives Canada Cataloguing in Publication

Grant, Vicki
Hold the pickles / Vicki Grant.
(Orca currents)

Issued in print and electronic formats.
ISBN 978-1-55469-920-9 (pbk.).—ISBN 978-1-55469-922-3 (pdf).—
ISBN 978-1-55469-923-0 (epub)

I. Title. II. Series: Orca currents
PS8613.R367H65 2012   jc813'.6   C2011-907541-5

First published in the United States, 2012
Library of Congress Control Number: 2011942579

Summary: Fifteen-year-old Dan Hogg gets a job as a hotdog mascot
at a food fair and finds himself caught up in another action-packed mystery.

MIX
Paper from
responsible sources
FSC® C016245

*Orca Book Publishers is dedicated to preserving the environment and has
printed this book on Forest Stewardship Council® certified paper.*

Orca Book Publishers gratefully acknowledges the support for its
publishing programs provided by the following agencies: the Government
of Canada through the Canada Book Fund and the Canada Council for the Arts,
and the Province of British Columbia through the BC Arts Council
and the Book Publishing Tax Credit.

Cover photography by Christopher Peterson / Getty Images
Author photo by Megan Tansey Whitton

ORCA BOOK PUBLISHERS
www.orcabook.com

Printed and bound in Canada.

20 19 18 17 • 6 5 4 3

*This book is dedicated
to Brennan Sarty, who kindly made
room in his costume for me.*

Chapter One

A hotdog.

No, it was worse than that. A *healthy* hotdog.

A six-foot, all-natural, high-fiber, low-fat, live-in wiener. I couldn't believe it.

When Uncle Hammy called to ask if I'd like to work for him at the Food Fantasia Fun Fair, I was actually kind of excited. I mean, who wouldn't be? The job offered the two things fifteen-year-old boys care most about in life: food and money.

All I had to do was hand out samples from his hotdog stand for an afternoon. I could eat as much as I wanted from the other food stalls *plus* he'd pay me ten bucks an hour.

Ten bucks an hour!

I couldn't believe my luck. Happy little money birds twittered around in my head. Up to that point, my luck had only come in one variety: rotten. Now it looked like something good was actually going to happen for me.

The offer came at exactly the right moment. Just before Hammy called, I'd been having a little "discussion" with my mother. I really, really needed a personal trainer, but she refused to pay for one. She wouldn't even talk about it.

"Dan," she said and laughed into her cup of coffee. "What do you need a personal trainer for?"

I'm sure the answer was obvious to everyone but her.

Girls. That's the other thing most fifteen-year-old boys care about. With the way I looked, though, I knew I didn't stand a chance with them. I couldn't do much about my glasses or my braces or my all-around nerdy vibe. But I figured I might be able to do something about my scrawny physique—or at least a paid professional could.

I did the math and took the job on the spot. If I worked the whole afternoon, I figured I could afford a couple of hours of training—maybe more. After all,

Hammy had mentioned the possibility of tips.

What he apparently forgot to mention—at least until I showed up at the Metro Center a week later, all ready to go—was that I had to wear a costume.

"I didn't tell you about that?" Hammy tried to sound innocent. "Funny. You wouldn't think I could forget something...*like this*!"

He whipped a giant pink-and-yellow foam hotdog out from behind his stall. Its rubbery arms flailed at me like a little kid in a fistfight.

My dork instinct immediately kicked in. I raised my hands up in front of my face for protection.

"It's not going to bite you," Hammy said. "It's a hotdog, Dan. If anything, *you* bite *it*." He had a good chuckle over that, but I didn't join in.

"You must be kidding. Wear *that*?" I brought my arms down and folded them across my so-called chest. "Forget it. Not a chance."

Hammy leaned against the hotdog and draped his hand over its sesame-seed shoulder as if they were long-lost brothers. The truth was, they did bear a remarkable resemblance to each other. They both had goofy grins, wiry red hair and mustard dribbling down their fronts. The only obvious difference was that the hotdog also came with relish.

Hammy picked up the hotdog's three-fingered hand and wagged it at me. "C'mon, Dan! Where's your sense of humor?"

Where's *my* sense of humor? This was the guy who decided to call himself "Hammy" because he thought it would be funny with the last name Hogg. Trust me, the name Hogg doesn't need any help getting laughs. I know that from personal experience.

"It's my dignity I'm worried about!" I said. "What would my friends say if they caught me parading around dressed like an enormous frankfurter?"

Hammy's face went serious. "I thought about that, actually. You know what I think they'll say?" He paused while he came up with an answer. "They'll say you look taller."

I glared at him. He knows I'm sensitive about my height.

"And stronger too!" Hammy held out one of the hotdog's arms. "Look. Built-in biceps!"

I rolled my eyes. "Yeah. Right. Like anyone is going to mistake those tennis balls for muscles."

"The kid's got no imagination either." Hammy seemed to be talking to the hotdog now. It gave him the same blank-eyed stare I did. "Oh well.

Doesn't matter," he said and patted me on the back. I relaxed.

"Phew," I said. Hammy always was a joker. "For a second there, I actually thought you were going to make me wear that stupid thing!"

That got the biggest laugh yet. "Course I am! I mean it doesn't matter what other people think. No one's going to see you. You'll be completely hidden. All they'll see is a big delicious Hogg's Dogg. Now let's get this show on the road! And by the way, you'd better strip down. It's hotter than a barbecue grill inside this thing."

Chapter Two

I wish I could say I turned and walked away, but I didn't. I did what I was told.

I stripped down to my tighty-whities, and Hammy slammed the hotdog over my head. I felt like a bumblebee trapped in a glass jar—except, of course, a bumblebee would at least have had a view. I could barely see a thing. I was supposed to look out through the black screens covering the hotdog's eyes, but as Hammy kindly pointed out, I wasn't tall enough. I had to stretch my neck even to peer out through the mouth.

Hammy helped me get my hands into the big white Mickey Mouse gloves and my feet into the giant green slippers that he claimed looked exactly like pickles. Then he ran me through my lines.

"Okay, Dan, try this. 'Hey, folks! You want fiber in your frankfurter? Then ask for me!'" He pointed his thumb at his chest. "'I'm Frank Lee Better. The Healthy Hottie! From Hawwwwwwwwwg's Doggs!'"

He sounded like he was calling down the next contestant on a TV game show.

The costume, the name, the stupid slogan—everything about this job was humiliating. I didn't need a personal trainer that bad.

So why was I doing it then?

I waddled from Hammy's food stall on Level D all the way down to the main exhibition floor. The metal braces that were supposed to keep my giant wiener head from wobbling dug into my shoulders. The tail end of my hotdog dragged on the cement floor. The rough edge of the foam cut into my armpits. The worst thing, though, was the bright blue *Frank Lee Better: Superhero* cape. Some superhero. I felt like I had a sign pinned to my back that said, *Make fun of me. I deserve it.*

At this point, a normal person would have packed up his self-respect and gone home. But I didn't. I hated everything about the job, but I couldn't let Hammy down. I knew his business was going through a rough patch. That's why he was trying out this new high-fiber hotdog. That's why he spent a thousand dollars for this dumb costume. He was desperate.

And it wasn't just because of business problems. The truth was, Hammy's whole *life* was going through a rough patch. First the divorce, then losing his house, then that weird thing that happened to his forehead after the hair-implant surgery. The guy seriously needed a break.

I figured we schmucks had to stick together. Who knows? Maybe a giant hotdog handing out samples for an afternoon would be enough to get people flocking to Hogg's Doggs. I could at least do that much for him.

And Hammy had been right about one thing. Unless someone recognized my scrawny ankles, no one would know who was inside the costume. At least I didn't have to worry about that.

I struggled to keep my pickle feet from slipping down the stairs and tried to be positive. I was sweating. I was straining. I was breathing hard.

This had to be good exercise at least. Some people got their workout in a gym. Some people got their workout in a pool. I just happened to get mine inside a giant hotdog.

That didn't sound as positive as I'd hoped.

Chapter Three

By the time I made it from Level D to the exhibition floor, half my samples had slid off my tray, and I was seriously hot. Sweat dripped down my back, and my glasses had steamed up like a shower door.

I could still see enough, though, to realize there were other mascots at the fair. In the crowd I spotted a drumstick, a sushi roll, a cupcake and at least three burgers. They were all hollering slogans and doing silly waves to attract customers. It was a relief to find out I wasn't the only person willing to make a fool of myself for a few bucks.

There was also plenty of real food. I remembered Hammy saying I could eat as many samples as I wanted. Suddenly the afternoon didn't seem that bad. I squinted out Frank's mouth to see what my choices were. The Codfather Fish 'n Chips looked good. I was dragging myself over to get in line when I had a terrible thought. How was I going to eat anything? The hotdog's mouth was a canoe-shaped grin covered in black mesh. There was nowhere to put the food.

I tried to slump in disappointment, but my wiener prison wouldn't even allow me to do that. I was trapped. My only option was to start handing out samples.

I didn't think I'd have many takers. All the other mascots had food that people would actually want to eat. My healthy hotties weren't hot anymore, and they sure didn't look too healthy. I didn't know if the added fiber turned them gray or if *all* wieners would look that sick without artificial color. I did know one thing though. There was no way I'd eat any—even if I had a mouth to do it with.

I stood on the sidelines, holding my tray out and occasionally muttering "Free samples." Everyone ignored me. I couldn't bring myself to do Hammy's whole dorky sales pitch. I did have *some* pride—although you'd never know it to look at me.

I was almost ready to give up when this kid stopped right in front of me.

He looked at my samples and said, "Ooh. Nice." I was hopeful for a second. Then he said, "Where'd you get those— the morgue?"

That was it. Something snapped inside me. I mean, these were *Hogg's* Doggs! No one could talk about my uncle's food like that! (Other than me, of course.)

I lowered my voice to make it as manly as I could. I sounded just like my Aunt Maxie. Then I hollered right in his ear, "I'll have you know you're talking to Frank Lee Better!"

I curled up one arm and pumped my tennis-ball bicep. "I'm all natural! High fiber! Low fat! I'm the best wiener on the market!"

The kid snorted, "Yeah, I bet you are," and left.

My rant hadn't worked as well as I'd wanted. It hadn't convinced the kid and had only managed to lure over one other customer, a little old lady. She held her purse with one hand and fingered the samples with the other.

"I'm just trying to find a nice warm one," she said in her sweet-little-old-lady voice. (As if that made her germs less deadly than the rest of ours.) She finally settled on an end piece with extra mustard.

She was sliding her glasses down to inspect it when I heard a girl's voice say, "These are all natural? Really? They look delicious!"

I waited for the punch line. My guess was that the other kid had sent someone over to torment me. I tipped my head back to get a better look and immediately realized I'd make a mistake. I had a lot more forehead than I usually did. The movement threw my balance off. I toppled over backward.

My pickled feet flew up in the air. My samples scattered. I landed hard on my sesame-seed bun. I worried for a second that everyone had seen my tighty-whities, and that's the last thing I remember.

Chapter Four

"Frank...? Frank?"

I blinked a few times, and this beautiful teenage girl appeared through the black screen of my goofy grin. She was leaning over me, looking into my eyes—or what she no doubt *thought* were my eyes. Her long brown hair swept across Frank's face. She was wearing pink lip gloss. She smelled like roses. It was almost too good to be true.

"Are you all right? Frank?"

She probably thought I was unconscious, but that wasn't the reason I didn't answer. The truth was, I was in shock. No one that good-looking had ever spoken to me in my entire life.

The old lady said, "Maybe we should call nine-one-one…"

My heart started pounding. I pictured paramedics pulling me out of the hotdog by my feet—and the beautiful girl realizing with horror that Frank Lee Better was actually Puny Little Me.

I couldn't let that happen.

"Ah…" I said.

"He's trying to talk!" She leaned in closer. I smelled her rose perfume again. That's when I remembered something really important.

I'm allergic to roses.

"Ah…" I went.

"Yes?" she said.

"Choo!" I let out a giant sneeze.

The blowback was so strong that my head bounced off the floor. Snot hit the inside of the hotdog and splattered back over my face and glasses.

The old lady scrunched up her lips and said, "Ooh. Must be awful messy in there."

The beautiful girl didn't shudder or move away from me in disgust. She just said, "Here. Let me help you." She took my Mickey Mouse hand and pulled me to my feet.

Beautiful, kind and really strong too. For a second there, I wondered who *her* personal trainer was. Maybe I should give him a call.

"You're very light for someone so tall," she said. I assumed she was joking, but then she handed me back my tray and added, "Must be all the healthy food you eat."

Was she for real? How hard had I hit my head? If I didn't have mucus dripping down my face, I would have thought I was dreaming.

"What a sin you lost all your samples." She shook her head. Her hair bounced around like it was starring in a shampoo commercial. "They look super yummy."

The old lady said, "Oh, yes! They certainly do," and took a bite of her sample. That took the smile off her face pretty fast. She made a *kekking* sound and put the rest of the hotdog back on the tray. Either the beautiful girl didn't notice, or she was too polite to mention it. The old lady held a hankie up to her mouth and toddled off fast.

I didn't know if I was thrilled to be alone with the beautiful girl or terrified. Probably a bit of both.

"So," she said, "do you make the hotdogs yourself? Is this your own company?"

I was about to say, "No, I'm only helping my uncle out," but then I thought, why would I say that? Why blow it? She thinks I'm tall, a business owner and obviously a lot older than I am. Who needed a personal trainer? I was starting to think dressing up as a hotdog was a much better way to get girls.

I said, "It's a family company," which was sort of the truth. An uncle is family.

"Really?" I could tell that impressed her. "It's so wonderful to see a company that truly cares about our health."

I was suddenly feeling way more confident. It was as if I'd actually become the person she thought I was.

"All these compliments are making me blush," I said in my Jolly Green Giant voice.

"You're kidding," she said and waved her hand at me.

"No, I'm not," I said. "See how I've gone all pink?" I pointed at my foam body.

She laughed like I'd just cracked the world's funniest joke. Then I really did blush.

My knees started to knock together. I went from sweating buckets to sweating rivers. I felt like I might faint. I was in love.

I was just thinking that this had to be the happiest day of my life when I heard a terrible sound. It was Shane Coolen screaming for a hotdog.

My love was doomed.

Chapter Five

That's not quite fair. I shouldn't say Shane Coolen is terrible. Not anymore at least. For years, he called me Pigboy and tortured me about my glasses and my teeth and stuff like that, but he's gotten nicer. We even kind of get along now.

That still didn't mean I was happy to hear his voice. I knew if he found out I was Frank Lee Better, he'd never be able to control himself. He's only human. He'd *have* to make fun of me. And that would be the end of my chances with the beautiful girl.

I told myself to calm down. How would Shane know it was me? The costume covered me right to my shins, and I hadn't used my real voice. As long as he didn't recognize the smell of my sweat, I figured I was okay.

"Don't move, Wienerboy! I mean it!" He came charging over with his big hand stretched out for the last sample. He didn't seem to notice there was a bite out of it. "Yes! I got it. I wanted a hotdog so bad, you wouldn't believe it."

He was about to put the sample in his mouth when he saw the girl. His hand stopped in midair.

"Well, hello there." He didn't even have to put on a Jolly Green Giant voice. It came natural to him.

I couldn't see the girl's face very well, but I could tell by the way she said hi that she was smiling.

I felt sick. She'd already made it clear that she liked tall, healthy guys, and Shane sure was tall and healthy. The kid had single-handedly lifted Mr. Benvie's SUV out of the snowbank last year. I assumed that was the only way he'd managed to pass geography. Shane didn't need to hide inside a foam hotdog to impress a girl.

"So, ah, what's your name?" He might have been tall and healthy, but Shane wasn't all that clever with the pickup lines.

"Brooke."

"You mean, like water?" He gave this lover-boy chuckle and winked at her. "I like water." I would have thrown up, but it was already gross enough inside the hotdog.

The worst thing was that the beautiful girl laughed at his joke just as hard as she'd laughed at mine. I told myself she was only being polite, but I didn't really believe it. Girls always laughed at Shane's jokes. There was just something about him they found cute. Frankly, I didn't understand the attraction, but that was probably fine with Shane.

He started talking as if I wasn't there. He asked Brooke if she'd like to get a bite to eat. He made it sound as if he was going to take her to some fancy restaurant instead of just walking over to a mascot with a trayful of free food.

She laughed again and said, "I don't know you very well." I got the impression that she'd like to change that. She reached out and touched his arm.

What was I thinking? Why would Brooke ever fall for six feet of foam

when she could have a real man—
or at least Shane?

He talked her into heading over to
check out what the dancing meatball
was offering. He still had my sample
in his hand.

"Let me finish this and…" He popped
it in his mouth, then made a sound like
a dog that had suddenly reached the
end of its leash. He started spitting and
sputtering and scraping at his tongue
with his fingernails.

"Ooh. Ugh. Gag. What *is* this?" He
looked at me as if I'd tried to poison
him. "It's disgusting!"

I didn't have a chance to reply. Shane
heaved and ran off with his hand over
his mouth.

"Oh, dear. Poor guy." Brooke watched
him disappear through the crowd. Her
big brown eyes looked sad. "He must
have gotten a bad one."

She was sympathetic, but she didn't run after him. I was amazed. Did she really prefer to stay with me? Even more amazing, I noticed that a second beautiful girl was there now too, standing beside Brooke. They could have been identical twins, except that this one had blond hair.

"Oh, Kelsey! I wondered where you were!" Brooke said. "You've got to meet Frank. He's so funny! You'll absolutely love him."

They both turned and smiled at me. I was making ten bucks an hour to talk to two beautiful girls who thought I was funny. I could barely breathe, I was so happy. It was as if, suddenly, everything in my life was going right. I didn't even feel like sneezing anymore.

But the good times didn't last very long.

I was just about to charm the girls with a few more of my witty remarks when I heard something even worse than Shane's voice.

Uncle Hammy's.

Chapter Six

"Hey, look, everybody! Isn't that Frank Lee Better?"

What was Uncle Hammy doing here? Why wasn't he manning his booth? I didn't want to turn around and find out.

"It is! It's the Healthy Hottie!" He was hollering like he'd just spotted Justin Bieber. People craned their necks to see. I can imagine how disappointed they were when they realized he was talking about a hotdog.

I had to stop Hammy before he said anything more. He was bound to humiliate me in front of Brooke—even if it was only by mentioning that he was my uncle.

I could hear him pound across the floor behind me. There was no time to waste.

"Excuse me," I said to the girls. "I've got to…"

"Oh, sorry," Brooke said, looking at Hammy. She had this perfect singsong voice. "Don't let us keep you from your fans!"

Kelsey swung her big red purse up onto her shoulder. "No. We wouldn't want to do that. That man looks like he's really excited to see you. You must be quite a celebrity!"

I couldn't tell if she was being sarcastic or not. I got the feeling she wasn't as nice as Brooke, but I didn't know why I thought that. It was something about her voice. It had an edge to it.

Hammy was hollering about my powerful biceps now and gaining on me. The girls' smiles had frozen on their faces. Their eyes shifted back and forth between me and Hammy. This was turning into one of those classic awkward moments that usually come right before the deeply embarrassing ones.

"I'll be right back," I said, then turned to cut Hammy off at the pass.

My cape swung up in the air just like a real superhero's would. I wondered if the girls thought it looked cool.

Or dorky?

Chapter Seven

First, the good news.

With so many people tromping through the hall, Hammy didn't notice his samples scattered all over the floor. He just saw my empty tray and must have thought they'd all been gobbled up by happy customers. He was thrilled.

"You're doing a great job, Frank! Or, should I say, *Dan*." He whispered as if my true identity was our little secret. "Boy. I'd better hurry back to my stall. Thanks to your stellar sales job, I bet there's a lineup by now!"

He handed me the new tray of samples he'd brought with him. "I won't be able to get down again until three. I doubt these will last until then..." He patted me on the back. "But do your best."

Now the bad news.

By the time I got rid of Hammy, I'd lost sight of the girls.

I wandered around the hall for ages with my head bent back so I could squint out the mouth hole. I didn't see them anywhere.

I decided to do my routine again. I yelled out, "I'm Frank Lee Better! The Healthy Hottie!" I wasn't embarrassed about doing it anymore. I had a purpose now. I figured if Brooke heard my voice, *she'd* come and find *me*.

The mere thought of that boosted my ego. She really did seem to like me.

Most people who heard my voice, though, clearly didn't. I got the usual reaction. I'd mention high fiber, and they'd turn and head for the nearest pizza stand. The few people who did take a sample didn't seem interested in finding out where they could get more. Hammy should have stuck to his old high-flavor recipe and not worried about nutrition. Nobody eats a hotdog for their health.

So that's why what happened next came as a surprise. I'd just finished my spiel and, naturally, expected everybody to keep walking by. Instead someone said, "Oh, what have we here?"

I turned toward the voice.

The next thing I knew, something whacked me hard in the ankles. My legs flew out from under me. Hammy's samples scattered all over the floor.

People ducked for cover. My head hit the ground. This was starting to feel like a bad habit.

I waited until the pain subsided before I opened my eyes. Call me crazy, but I was hoping to see Brooke leaning over me again. The concussion would have been worth it.

Unfortunately, that's not what happened.

I saw a giant yellow cupcake wearing a thick coat of white icing and a jaunty cherry hat. It batted its long black eyelashes at me.

"Oh, sorry. Are you okay?" The cupcake had a little girly voice.

I groaned and got halfway up on my elbows. "Yeah. I'm fine," I said, although the world seemed to be spinning all of a sudden.

"Careful! You lie back down now." The cupcake gently pushed me onto the floor. "You could still be dizzy. You might hurt yourself."

The pink smile on its spongy face didn't change, but the voice sure did. "Listen, meathead," it whispered into an eyehole in a deep rumble. "Beat it. This is Cupcake Katie territory. Show your buns around here again, and I'll shove each and every one of those sesame seeds down your high-fiber throat. Understand?"

He yanked me onto my feet, and I heard my cape tear. The creep actually laughed. "Oops. How did that happen?" he said. "Didn't realize I was standing on it. Silly me…"

Normally, you'd think a hotdog could take on a cupcake, but this guy wasn't your average cupcake.

Or your average Katie.

It was safer to get out of there while I could. I was a little ashamed of myself. I had the feeling an all-beef frankfurter wouldn't let himself be pushed around like that.

Cupcake Katie did a little dance and waved a yellow glove at me. "Toodle-oo, Frank Lee! Hope you're feeling better," he said in the girly voice. I wanted to punch him right in his muffin-top, but I knew when I was beat.

I got as far away from him as I could. Once I was safe, I had a twinge of guilt about ruining Hammy's expensive costume. But my guilt didn't last long. I had something else on my mind.

Brooke.

Sooner or later I was going to have to step out of this hotdog and show her the real me. Let's face it, the real me couldn't stand up to a miniature marshmallow, let alone a full-size cupcake with attitude. I didn't know how she'd react to sad little Dan Hogg. It made me nervous. But what could I do about it? I just kept hoping that if

I really put the charm on, she'd still like me when the ugly truth finally came out.

But where was I going to find her?

I wandered around the hall, but it seemed useless. I couldn't do my sales pitch with no samples to give away. The costume was getting heavier all the time. And I didn't even know if Brooke was still here. She might have eaten her fill and gone home by now.

I was starting to feel depressed about the whole situation when I spotted Shane cramming his pockets full of samples from Eat-o-Burrito's.

Half an hour earlier I'd been thrilled to get rid of the guy. Now he seemed like the only person who could help me find Brooke. I cleared my throat and headed over.

"Excuse me, sir," I said in a deep voice. "A little while ago, you were speaking with a dark-haired girl over by The Codfather Fish 'n Chips stand. I wonder if you might know where she is."

Shane wiped a dribble of salsa off his chin with his sleeve and said, "Yeah. Maybe. Why do you want to know, Dan?"

Chapter Eight

I thought I was going to fall over again.

"How did you know it was me?" I said in my normal voice.

Shane pounded his chest with his fist and dislodged a greasy burp. "Oh, please," he said. "Who else has ankles that skinny?"

"You recognized me by my ankles?"

"Yeah." He shrugged. "Well, that and the Hogg's Doggs thing. I just put two and two together."

I wanted to say, "*You* can put two and two together?" but a guy dressed like a hotdog really shouldn't tease anyone about anything. "So why didn't you mention it?" I said.

"In front of that Brooke girl?" Shane squinted one eye and shook his head. "I didn't want to embarrass you. I have a heart, you know."

That would have been touching, if he hadn't chosen that exact moment to yank a wiry red hair out of Frank Lee's head and use it to pick something from between his back teeth.

"Ah, gee, thanks, Shane," I said. "So...I, ah, don't suppose you know where she is now, do you?"

He shoved another Burrito-Bit in his mouth. "Nah. I don't. But I wouldn't tell you even if I did."

So much for Mr. Nice Guy.

"How come?" I said.

"I told ya! I have a heart. I wouldn't want you to get your hopes up."

"What are you talking about?"

"Dan. It was so obvious. The way you shuffled around in your little green shoes." He did a short demonstration to make sure I got the point. "And put on that lame superhero voice. You obviously liked her. But let's be frank, Dan. Brooke's more my type of girl. We both know it."

He put his beefy arm around me and squeezed. I assumed he didn't realize he was cutting off the oxygen supply to my brain. "Don't be upset, old buddy. You'll find someone. Who knows? There's probably a nice little female meatball or chicken nugget prancing around here today who'd love to get to know a guy like you."

I tried not to be insulted. I don't

think Shane meant it in a mean way, but he clearly didn't think I was much of a ladies' man. What guy longs to meet the meatball of his dreams?

Shane slapped me on the back. That at least forced some air back into my lungs. "I'm only joking," he said. "There is something serious I'd like to talk to you about though."

"Oh yeah? What?" Even heartbroken, I was kind of interested. I don't think I'd ever heard Shane say anything serious.

"Don't suppose you'd lend me ten bucks, would you? I can't seem to find my wallet. I don't know what the matter is with these guys, but no one'll give me any more freebies."

Chapter Nine

There was no way I believed Shane had lost his wallet, but I didn't say so. I didn't have to. I could honestly tell him I didn't have any money to lend. I mean, where would Frank Lee Better put a wallet? Hotdog buns generally didn't come with pockets or man-purses—thank goodness. Shane insisted on frisking me anyway but eventually gave up and wandered off to find another victim.

To tell the truth, I almost missed Shane when he was gone. I had nothing to do. No samples to give away, no girls to charm. I was even afraid to move very far, because Cupcake Katie hadn't bothered to show me where his territory began. I didn't want to stumble into enemy hands.

I was wandering aimlessly past the Flab-U-Less Lo-Cal Pizza stand when someone grabbed me.

"Frank! It's me!"

That voice, that beautiful voice. Brooke had found *me*! I was so happy, I didn't mind that her perfume instantly clogged up my sinuses again.

This wasn't a joyful reunion though. Something was wrong.

"Don't let him see me," she said. I couldn't see her face, but I could tell she was upset. "Please. Hide me."

"Let *who* see you, Brooke? What's the matter? Are you all right?"

"Shh!" she said, then slipped behind me and under my ripped cape. I could feel her shaking. Was Cupcake Katie after her too?

I felt bad that Brooke was upset, but I felt good too. I mean, she came to *me* for help. So much for me not being her type, Shane! Where was he when she needed him? Huh?

A guy dressed in blue hurried by, then stopped a few steps away from me. He put his hands on his hips and looked around as if he was trying to see what smelled bad.

Or maybe, to see what smelled *good*. Had he noticed Brooke's perfume?

He turned around and walked right up to me. I didn't like the look of this guy at all. Next to him, Cupcake Katie seemed like a mildly irritated lunchroom monitor.

Brooke wasn't just shaking now, she was downright rattling. I was doing a bit of that myself, although I tried my best to control it.

Blue Boy tilted his head to one side as if he was trying to see behind me. I leaned over too and struck a kind of bent-superhero pose. "Why, hello there, sir! I'm Frank Lee Better!" I was doing my best to distract him.

He waved me away with his hand. "Yeah, yeah, whatever. Cut the crap, kid."

"Crap!" I said. I made my voice as loud as I could and stood on my tiptoes to look taller. People turned to see what was going on. "I'm the Superhero Hotdog!" I boomed. "You know what they say. Frank Lee Better is Frank Lee the Best. I can leap high buildings...break big sticks...carry large pots of water..."

I was making it up as I went along, but I was running out of things to say. (I don't think well under pressure, and believe me, having a beautiful girl hiding under your cape is stressful. Nice, but stressful.) As it turned out, I didn't need to come up with much more.

I wasn't sure if it was because I was shaking so much or if someone accidentally knocked me from behind, but I lost my balance again. My arms shot straight out in front of me. An image of Superman taking off into the air flashed through my mind. Then I fell forward like the giant foam hotdog that I was.

I landed right on top of the guy.

People started to laugh and clap. They must have thought it was some kind of publicity stunt.

For one nanosecond I was glad the guy was there to cushion my fall. Then reality struck.

By which I mean the guy struck.

He whacked me in the side of the head and said, "Get off me, you idiot!"

As if I was doing this on purpose. I didn't like the situation any more than he did.

I tried to move, but it wasn't easy. My arms barely touched the ground, and I couldn't see at all. The guy's sleeve was blocking Frank's mouth hole. I didn't know where to put my hands to push myself up. I just lay on top of the guy and flailed away with my arms as if I was paddling out to sea on a bad-tempered surfboard.

The guy finally exploded. He got me by the hair and threw me aside like a dirty blanket. He stood up, grabbed me by my armpits and pulled me up too. I heard my cape rip again, but I wasn't that worried about it. I was more worried about what he was planning to do to the rest of me.

He was so mad, his face was scrunched up like a weightlifter's. He looked me in the eyes—or at least what he thought were my eyes—and said, "You okay?"

I was shocked. Why was he suddenly worried about my health? I figured there were too many people around for him to say what he really wanted to say.

I managed to croak out, "Yes."

He poked me in the chest—or at least what he thought was my chest but was actually my chin. Then he whispered, "Well, you won't be if you get in my way again."

His eyes were bloodshot. He was spraying spit. He was threatening to clobber me for accidentally knocking him over. No wonder Brooke was afraid of him.

"You think you're pretty funny, don't you?" Normally I'd admit that I did, but that wasn't the answer he was looking for. "Listen here…"

Like I had a choice! He was stepping on one of my pickles. I wasn't going anywhere.

"You cross my path again and, so help me, I'll wipe that stupid grin off your face! They won't be able to use what's left of you to *make* hotdogs. You understand? Now get out of here, before I do something I could regret."

Wow, I thought. They call this place a Fun Fair? I hadn't been threatened with this much violence since Shane and I were in elementary school together.

I nodded.

"Have a nice day," he said and stormed off. The guy had serious mood issues, but that wasn't what upset me the most.

I looked around.

Brooke was gone again.

I couldn't help feeling I'd let her down. She should have known better than to rely on a wimp like me for protection.

Chapter Ten

I was hungry, sweaty, worried and scared. Somehow the ten dollars an hour I was going to make didn't seem like that good a deal anymore.

If I even made the money, that is.

On top of everything now, I was afraid of what Uncle Hammy would do when he saw the cape. He'd paid a thousand dollars for this costume.

He was bound to be upset. My mother always said, "There's nothing worse than an angry Hogg." That almost scared me more than Cupcake Katie or Blue Boy did.

I realized I couldn't let Uncle Hammy pay me. It wouldn't be right. I'd torn the costume *and* I'd barely even managed to hand out any samples. Some spokeswiener I turned out to be.

I decided to cut my losses and give the costume to Hammy right away before I totally ruined it. Maybe if I helped him clean up at the end of the day, he'd forgive me.

I waddled toward the exit. I was tired, so I was moving slowly. But I also needed time to figure out what to say to Hammy. I wasn't looking forward to the conversation at all.

I had just passed Bubble Tea 'n Biscuits when someone grabbed my hand and pulled me behind the stall.

Not this again, I thought.

"Frank!"

My heart skipped numerous beats. Brooke hadn't given up on me after all.

She didn't let go of my hand, even when she turned and called out in a loud whisper, "Kelsey! I found him!"

Brooke waved Kelsey over, then turned back to me. "We've been looking everywhere for you! I wanted to thank you for rescuing me."

She put her arms around me and kissed my cheek—or at least what she thought was my cheek. I was so thrilled, I forgot to sneeze.

"It was nothing," I said, and I meant it—although I tried to make it sound like I was just being humble. If she wanted to think I was heroic for falling over at the right time, why should I argue?

"Nothing?!" she said in disbelief. "No, it wasn't, was it, Kelsey?"

Kelsey stopped rummaging around in her big red purse and looked at me. "It was totally a big deal," she said. She gave a quick smile, then went back to rifling through her stuff.

"See?" Brooke said. "I told you. I'm so glad you were there for me. That guy has been following me around all day. He gives me the creeps."

He gave me the creeps too, but I didn't say so. I said, "Would you like me to call security about him for you?" I hoped that sounded like a mature response to the situation.

Brooke shook her head and chuckled as if I was being silly. It was very cute. "Oh, no! I'd never do that to the poor guy! He's harmless."

He didn't look harmless to me. I didn't mention that though. I didn't want to sound like a wimp.

"He's probably just lonely." She shrugged. "It's sort of my fault that he's hanging around. I should have been firmer with him in the first place, but I didn't want to hurt his feelings. I thought it would be mean to say I wasn't interested in him. It might have been nicer to tell him that, though, than to hide every time he comes by now!"

She laughed and fiddled with the green-felt relish sewn to my front. It reminded me of my mother fixing my father's tie before he got his picture taken.

"I guess that's one thing you don't have to worry about, eh?" she said.

"Him being interested in me?" I said.

Brooke laughed like I was making a joke, but I honestly didn't know what she was talking about.

"No, silly! Having to hide!" She tried to look into my eyeholes. "You're totally disguised in this big old thing. I don't even know what you look like!"

Now *that* really scared me. I stepped away.

"Oh, I'm nothing special," I said. "Just your average ruggedly handsome movie-star type. You know."

She laughed again and gave me a little push. Then she paused like she was embarrassed.

"What?" I said.

She bit her lip, and her eyes lit up.

"What?" I said again. "You can tell me."

"Oh, I don't know. I was just thinking it must be fun to wear a costume."

I was going to tell her that, in fact, it's not. The costume is hot and sticky and awkward, and thanks to some unfortunate allergies, it was also covered in snot. But I decided against it. I didn't want to gross her out. I also didn't want to sound like I was whining.

"Oh, yeah!" I said. "It's really fun. You get to try on a whole new personality when you wear one of these."

That at least was true.

"And you see things from an entirely different point of view too." Again true.

"Wow. Neat," she said. I don't think a girl had ever responded to me with either of those words. "You get to goof around and do those funny dances, don't you?"

"Oh, yeah," I said, although to me that seemed like a definite downside of the job.

"Show us," she said.

I hoped she was joking.

"Come on!" she said and clapped her hands. Kelsey joined in too. "Come on!"

I'm not much of a dancer. I haven't had a lot of opportunity. None of the girls ever lined up to boogie with me at the school dances. But Brooke wanted me to do it, so I did my best.

I just shuffled my feet—the type of thing an itchy duck might do—

but the girls laughed and laughed. That encouraged me to wiggle my bun and spin my hands around a bit too. It must have been funnier than I thought it was.

"Oh, my gosh. That's hysterical!" Brooke had to wipe the tears from her eyes. "Mind if I try?"

I wasn't sure I heard her right.

"Could I try on the costume?"

She took one of my hands in both of hers and looked me right in the eyes—or at least what she thought were my eyes.

"Could I? Please? You make it look like so much fun. Just for a minute? I won't go far. Please?"

Everything told me to say no. Uncle Hammy would get mad. I had no clothes to put on. The costume was wet and slimy inside. Brooke would find out that it wasn't the least bit fun to be a mascot.

But she smiled at me and clasped her hands in front of her and jumped up and down a bit too, so none of that stuff mattered.

"Sure," I said. "Why not?"

Chapter Eleven

It took me at least ten minutes to get out of the costume. It was slimy inside, so I couldn't get a good enough grip to pull it over my head. I finally just lay facedown on the floor of the men's washroom and slithered out backward. It must have looked like the birth of an earthworm.

I stood up and caught a glimpse of myself in the mirror. I actually looked even worse than before. I was still short and skinny and dressed in my underwear, of course. But I was also bright pink and dripping in sweat now too. I had a heat rash on my chin and waxy speckles of snot on my glasses. I'm sure Brooke would have found a newborn earthworm more attractive than me.

Brooke knocked on the washroom door, and I actually jumped like a baby kangaroo. I even had my hands clenched in front of my chest like paws. That's how scared I was. I knew it would be game over if Brooke saw me like this.

"Sorry. I'm not quite ready yet," I said in the manliest way I could.

She groaned in kind of a jokey way and said, "Oh, no! What's taking you so long?"

"Ah...Well, let's just say, technical difficulties." They were snot-related technical difficulties, but she didn't need to know that.

"Well, hurry up, Frank! I really want to do this."

I could tell she was excited to try on the costume, but there was no way I was going to let her have it yet. The Dan Hogg fumes would have killed her. I had to disinfect it first.

It took me a good ten minutes. I completely scrubbed down the costume with pink hand soap, then dried it off with paper towel. It was a lot of work. Wearing a costume means you have to worry about twice as many armpits as you usually do.

Brooke knocked again. "Coming!" I said and gave Frank one more quick check. (And I'm glad I did. There was a wet noodle of snot still hanging from the mouth hole.) I positioned myself behind the door so she couldn't see me and pushed the costume through.

"Oh, thank you, Frank! This is going to be so much fun! Don't worry! I'll be back soon!"

"Whoa. Wait. Don't forget the slippers," I said and handed them out the door.

"No, no, that's fine. I'll just wear my own shoes. Here, Kelsey. Help me get this on!" I heard their footsteps fade. I peeked through the door in time to see the girls disappear into the ladies' washroom.

I sat in the cubicle for about five minutes feeling blissfully happy. It's not often that a guy like me gets to make a beautiful girl's dream come true.

Then I sat in the cubicle for five minutes more, feeling not quite so happy. Brooke must have lost track of time, I thought. She said she'd be right back.

Then I sat for about two minutes more, feeling downright terrified. Something wasn't right. Brooke was gone too long. It must have been about two thirty by then.

Two thirty!

That's when I remembered Hammy saying he'd be down at three o'clock with fresh samples. I started to shake. He'd paid big money for that costume. I was pretty sure I wasn't supposed to be lending it out. What would he do if he realized I wasn't inside it?

I knew the answer.

Hammy wasn't going to be an Angry Hogg if he caught me. He'd be more like a Wild Boar. (I'd seen the nature videos. This wasn't going to be pretty.)

I did jumping jacks for a while to try and keep my anxiety under control, but they didn't help. They just made me all sweaty again.

I looked out the door at least fifteen times. Brooke had promised she wouldn't go far, but I couldn't see her anywhere. My imagination went crazy. Maybe she fainted from the heat. Maybe she'd gotten disoriented.

Maybe the guy in blue had abducted her.

I could see my heart pounding through my skinny chest. I was really scared. Brooke shouldn't have been so relaxed about that guy. He was bad. I knew it right from the start. I should have called security like I said I was going to.

I had to find Brooke. But how? She was somewhere in a giant arena full of people.

And I was stuck in the men's room in nothing but my underwear and a pair of big green slippers that supposedly looked just like pickles.

Chapter Twelve

Sit in a washroom cubicle long enough, and a janitor is bound to come in. He'll usually be pushing a cart full of mops and brooms and cleaning supplies. He might be whistling the type of song your grandfather whistles—something loud and happy but without much of a tune.

If you're small and quiet, and of course desperate, you can sometimes hide until the janitor is busy trying to unclog one of the toilets. Then you can sneak behind him, grab a giant garbage bag from his cart and slip back into your cubicle unnoticed.

At least that's what I found.

I waited until the janitor left the washroom, then took off my slippers and climbed into the garbage bag. This was a new low even for me.

I yanked out a mile or two of paper towel and stuffed it around me. I wanted the bag to look full.

Now came the hard part.

I pulled the bag up to my shoulders and ducked my head inside. I fit— but just barely. I poked my hands out through the sides and tied a knot in the top of the bag. It was pretty sloppy, so I could break out if I needed to. I pulled my arms back in. I used my thumbs to make two big eyeholes and then, just to be safe, a whole bunch of airholes too.

I bounced over to the door. By the time I got there, my knees were killing me. If I ever wanted to walk again, this wasn't going to work.

Luckily, I hadn't cut my toenails in a while. I used the sharp edges to make two more big holes in the bottom of the bag and wiggled my feet out. I must have looked like an egg about to hatch.

I stuck a hand out and opened the door. I checked to make sure the coast was clear, then waddled outside.

My plan was to be as inconspicuous as possible. I figured no one would notice another garbage bag—as long as the garbage bag didn't go and do something stupid, of course.

I crouched against the wall and inched my way toward the main hall. I tried to keep my toes tucked under the belly of the bag. (I also tried not to squeal when I stepped on cold, mushy French fries, but it wasn't easy.) Nobody pointed at me or screamed in shock. Everyone was more focused on the free samples than on garbage.

Whenever I came to a trash can or a vending machine, I hid behind it for a break. Crouching was hard on the legs. And garbage bags are even hotter than foam wieners.

I was catching my breath behind an overflowing trash can when I found Brooke. I heard her before I saw her. "I'm Frank Lee Better! All natural! High fiber!" She'd lowered her voice so she sounded kind of like a guy.

I stretched the eyeholes open a bit more so I could get a good look.

I was so relieved—not only to find her, but to see her doing such a good job. She didn't have any samples to give away, but people still crowded around her, all dying to find out more about Hogg's Doggs. Maybe Hammy wouldn't be mad after all.

Kelsey was there too. She hovered at the edge of crowd like she was just another bystander. As usual, she was rooting around in that big purse of hers. Something about it irritated me. It was like a person texting someone else while they were supposed to be talking to you. She should have been paying more attention to her friend.

"C'mon, folks. Don't be shy," Brooke said. "Step right up. Let me tell you all about the Healthy Hottie!"

It almost seemed wrong to stop her. She was doing so much better than I ever had. I looked up and checked the big clock in the middle of the hall. It was only two forty. Hammy wouldn't be here for a while.

I was trying to decide if I should wait here or go back to the washroom when the decision was made for me. I heard whistling. It was loud and happy, but without much of a tune.

The janitor.

I looked out the eyeholes.

He had his cart with him. He was emptying the trash cans.

My first thought was to stay where I was and let him throw me in his cart. I'd wait until his back was turned, then make my escape.

I watched him toss a bag into his cart, and two things struck me: a) that would hurt, and b) there was no way my bag would survive the flight. It was too full of holes. It was bound to burst apart and send me and my tighty-whities flying across the room.

The janitor might also get suspicious of a garbage bag that weighed ninety-seven pounds. That was the first and only time in my life I wished I weighed less.

I had to do something fast. The janitor was getting closer. That happy song was starting to sound like the soundtrack to a horror movie.

I did the only thing I could think of. I climbed out of the garbage bag and hid behind a trash can.

I realized pretty fast that wouldn't work either. The janitor would pick up the half-empty bag of paper towel, and then he'd pick up the trash can and empty it.

So much for my hiding place.

So much for my life.

Chapter Thirteen

I had pretty much accepted that I was going to die of embarrassment at the ripe old age of fifteen when—just like that—my salvation appeared right in front of me.

Cupcake Katie.

He was striding past my hiding place, chatting away with a large burrito all gussied up in a sombrero and extra cheese. I'd like to say it was my lightning-fast mind that found the solution to my problem, but it wasn't. It was more like mascot's intuition or something. I just stood up straight and slipped in between the two of them. I knew they'd never be able to see me through their little pretend eyes. Their foam bodies were big enough that I was pretty much hidden from everyone too.

Even better, they just happened to be heading to the men's room. Miracle of miracles. I got all the way there with them unnoticed, then slipped into my old cubicle before they had a chance to get out of their costumes. I crouched on the toilet seat so they couldn't see my bare legs. If Shane had been able to recognize me by my ankles, why couldn't the cupcake?

I knew I was still in a bad situation, but this kind of took the edge off it.

There was something just so great about being able to use Cupcake Katie to make my getaway. I was feeling pretty smug—at least until they started to talk.

"You hear the news?" I figured that had to be the burrito, because I didn't recognize the voice.

"No. What?"

"Pickpockets."

"You're kidding." Cupcake Katie didn't sound that impressed. "Does my icing look like it's on straight to you?"

The burrito raised his voice over the sound of running water. "Push it a little to the left...Yeah. There. You got it."

"Have they caught anyone?"

"Not yet. But I've got a pretty good idea who's doing it."

"Oh, yeah. Who?"

"That lame hotdog."

My ears perked up. No, I thought. They couldn't possibly be talking about *me*.

The burrito went on, "You know. The one that tried to horn in on your territory? Frank Lee Awful or Frank Lee Inedible or something like that."

They had a laugh over that. I, on the other hand, almost had a heart attack.

Cupcake Katie said, "No way. He wouldn't pickpocket anyone." I was flattered that he came to my defense. "He's too much of a klutz! Didn't you see? I barely touched him, and he went down like a rock."

I heard a strip of paper towel being ripped off.

"No, no. You don't understand." It was the burrito again. "He doesn't actually *do* the pickpocketing. He's the decoy."

"What do you mean?"

"He lures the people over with the samples, then his 'associates' pick their pockets."

The cupcake snorted. "He'd get a lot more victims if he had samples you could actually eat."

Good point. I hoped that would put an end to this ridiculous discussion.

"Yeah—but that's what's so great about his plan. The guy's a lot smarter than he looks. His samples are so revolting that all anyone can think is, 'Get this out of my mouth!' They're not worrying about their wallets. You could rob them blind, and they wouldn't care."

"Brilliant," Cupcake Katie said. "I mean, in a sick sort of way. The hotdog must be raking in the money. Did you see the pile of people he had when we walked by just now?"

"Yeah. I wouldn't be surprised if the owner's in on it too. He's so hard up these days, he'd take money any way he can. Last week he tried to talk me into working for him, but I said no way. He only offered to pay ten bucks an hour! Can you believe it?"

"Ten bucks an hour? You're kidding! That's highway robbery. I wouldn't do it for anything less than twenty."

"Me neither...Oh well. Look at the time, would ya? It's quarter to three. Better get going."

"Yeah...Whoa, José. You got some toilet paper stuck to the bottom of your shoe."

They walked out the door. The last thing I heard was the burrito saying, "Next time I see that security guard, I'm going to tell him to go after the wiener. Guys like that should be in jail."

Chapter Fourteen

I sat on the toilet. Without that hot, sticky garbage bag, I was shivering. Could this day get any worse? The burrito was going to run to the security guard with his ridiculous theory. Next thing I'd know, Hammy and Brooke would be dragged to the police station in chains.

I'd feel bad about Hammy, but I'd feel worse about Brooke. She was prettier. But that wasn't the only reason. She seemed so innocent. She was just some poor girl who wanted to have a bit of fun.

I pictured Brooke in the hotdog costume dancing around. Then another image popped into my head. I saw Kelsey circling the crowd—Kelsey, who was always rummaging around in her big red purse.

The burrito's words came back to me. *His associates pick their pockets.* I got a sick feeling. It dawned on me that his theory might not be that crazy after all.

There was something about Kelsey I didn't like right off the bat. She was different from Brooke. Somehow, I just knew she had to be behind this. What was she putting in that purse of hers?

I remembered something else. Shane asking me for money. That in itself wasn't unusual—Shane was just that kind of guy. But he'd said he'd lost his wallet. What if he was wrong? What if it had been stolen?

I thought back. He'd taken a sample from me and then run off to spit it out. That was the first time I met Kelsey. She must have been right behind him. With Shane focused on food and a pretty girl, it probably wasn't that hard to take his wallet out of his back pocket without him noticing. It all fit.

I bit my knuckles. What had I done? I was supposed to be helping Uncle Hammy in his time of need. Instead, I'd torn the thousand-dollar costume, thrown his samples all over the floor and somehow made it look like he was the kingpin of a pickpocket racket. (Not an easy thing to do, considering I'm talking about Hammy Hogg.)

Now Brooke was mixed up in this too.

I shouldn't have lied to her. I should have told her how horrible it was inside the costume. Then she never would have put it on. She never would have found herself in this mess.

If the burrito got a chance to talk to the security guard, I was going to be in big trouble. We were all going to be in big trouble.

I couldn't let that happen.

I stuck my head out the washroom door. The hall was still crowded with people. I scanned the room for signs of Brooke. I was worried I'd never find her, but then, bingo! I spotted Frank's blue cape. Brooke was leaning against the wall near the Bison Burger stand. It looked like she was taking a rest.

"Psst! Brooke!" I called to her, but she didn't turn around. She must have been too far away to hear. I wondered where Kelsey was. Maybe she was using someone else as a decoy now.

If I could warn Brooke to get out of the costume, I might still be able to save her.

"Brooke!" I was practically screaming.

She didn't move, but a number of other people turned around. That's when it dawned on me. The last thing in the world I wanted was for Brooke to see me in my underwear. Yes, I wanted to save her, but I didn't want to blow my chances with her when I did.

I tried to think of a way out of my predicament. I couldn't use this garbage-bag getup anymore. I had to be able to reach her fast without her seeing what I looked like. I noticed toilet paper on the floor. That must have been the bit that was stuck to the burrito's shoe.

That gave me an idea. I stepped out of the garbage bag and got to work.

Chapter Fifteen

Sometimes a man's gotta do what a man's gotta do.

I grabbed the end of a roll of toilet paper. I started at my forehead and kept winding and winding and winding the tissue around myself until I got to my toes. I went through three rolls. I poked holes for my nostrils and wrapped it around my biceps a few extra times just so they didn't look so scrawny. I thought I may as well impress Brooke while I had the chance.

I stood back and looked at myself in the mirror. I probably should have put my glasses *over* the toilet paper not under it. They made a weird lump in the middle of my face, but still...I had to give myself credit. Considering what I had to work with, this wasn't a bad disguise.

I'd just thrown the empty tubes of toilet paper in the trash can when the door banged open and a guy rushed in.

The guy.

The there-won't-be-enough-of-you-left-to-make-hotdogs guy.

Blue Boy.

He looked me up and down. For a second, I thought he recognized me, but then he said, "You some kind of mascot or something?"

"Ah. Yeah," I said. This was working out better than I thought it was going to.

"What for?"

"Mummy's Home Cooking." It just came to me. I thought it was pretty clever, but Blue Boy looked like he didn't believe me. "You've heard of us, of course," I said. "Everyone's dying to try our, ah, Pharoah's Phries." I nudged him with my elbow, but he didn't laugh. He squinted at me suspiciously and said, "Well, okay…" as if this was a test and I just barely passed.

He started kicking open the cubicles like he was a narc on a drug raid, and I darted out the door. The guy was clearly crazy. I would have run out of there even if I didn't have something important to do.

I slowed down once I was back in the hall. I didn't want to draw attention to myself. I'd also wrapped the toilet paper on a little tighter than I should have. It was already starting to tear. I had to focus on getting to Brooke.

Most of the people I passed ignored me, but one little girl said, "Why's that guy all covered in toilet paper, Mommy?"

"Shush, Tyler," her mother said. "He must be ill."

Maybe my disguise wasn't as good as I thought it was, but it didn't matter. Brooke was right in front of me now, still leaning against the wall by the Bison Burger.

I was happy until I realized I didn't know what I was going to say to her. She couldn't find out it was me. She wasn't the type of girl who would fall for some dork wrapped in bathroom tissue. I decided to play dumb.

"Excuse me, would you happen to be Brooke?" I said. I was going to tell her I was a friend of Frank's and had a message for her. She didn't answer.

"Brooke?" I said.

That's when I noticed she wasn't leaning against the wall. She was *slumped* against the wall, as if she was unconscious. That scared me. I knew how hot it got inside that costume. She could have fainted or gotten sick.

"Brooke?" Still no answer. Maybe that soap I used was toxic. I slapped my hand against my chest, and my elbow ripped through my toilet paper sleeve.

I leaned down to see if she was all right. I could smell her rose perfume.

"Brooke...? Are you all right? Brooke?" I gave her a little shake.

The costume was empty.

Chapter Sixteen

I don't know if it was the rose perfume or the shock of finding out that Brooke was gone, but my body reacted. I jerked forward and sneezed so hard that I tore the face and bum right out of my costume. It was pretty much toast after that.

The impact knocked Frank to the ground. I saw with horror that his whole left side was covered in dirt and ketchup (not his own).

A thousand bucks. That's what I kept thinking. Poor Hammy.

Poor me.

I looked at the big clock in the middle of the hall. *2:58*. Despite all his faults, Hammy was always on time. He would be here any minute. I instinctively turned toward the stairs to check if I was too late.

I didn't see Hammy, but I saw something else.

A big red purse.

I squinted through the crowd. Yes. That was Kelsey's purse. Over by the exit. I stood on my tippy toes. Kelsey was talking to someone. He turned toward me.

It was Shane.

He moved his big square head, and I saw that Brooke was there too. She had her hand on his arm and was laughing.

With all the trouble I was in and all the trouble I was *going* to be in, I should have been worrying about more important things than whether a girl liked me or not. But I wasn't. All I could think was, Brooke's laughing at one of Shane's jokes.

It broke my heart. As if on cue, the bit of toilet paper still clinging to my hips slid to the floor. Standing there in my underwear, I couldn't deny it any longer. Shane really was more Brooke's type than I was.

I heard the squeal of a door opening and turned around. Blue Boy came barreling out of the washroom and was running right for me. He was talking into his shoulder, just like they do in the movies.

I suddenly understood.

The outfit. The beefy build. Kicking the cubicles open. This guy *was* the security guard.

I turned again and saw Hammy, right on schedule, walking through the middle of the crowd. He had fresh samples on his tray and a big grin on his face.

I read somewhere that when a person is in the middle of a disaster, things happen in slow motion. I can now say for a fact that it's one-hundred-percent true.

Everything wound down. The sound turned off. I saw the world clearly.

The security guard was going to arrest me, either for pickpocketing or public nudity or both. Hammy was going to watch it happen and then get arrested too. So was Brooke. For one brief moment I pictured the two of us, together at last. I was almost looking forward to it until I realized the paddy wagon probably wasn't the best place to start a relationship. Meanwhile, Kelsey was going to walk out the door with all the money in her big red purse.

The security guard kept charging toward me. His arms were pumping. His mouth was stretched back toward his ears from the effort. Sweat sprayed off his forehead in a sparkling silver arc. I even had time in my slow-motion world to think that it looked kind of pretty.

I can explain everything to the security guard, I thought.

No, I decided, it would take too long to convince him. Kelsey would be gone by then.

I had to get the purse myself. I needed evidence.

I looked at the Frank Lee Better costume. I realized it was too late put it on. I realized I was going to have to run through the crowded hall in my one-hundred-percent-cotton, Y-front briefs. I realized I had no other choice.

It was a split-second decision. I bolted out ahead of the security guard. The few remaining squares of toilet paper flew off my shoulders like autumn leaves off a speeding car. People looked at me and laughed. I didn't slow down. I kept going, even when I knocked a mascot called Sushi Sue right onto her wasabi.

Kelsey heard the commotion and turned around. She probably didn't know what hit her. I yanked her big red purse off her shoulder and picked up speed. She screamed, "Help! Help! Thief!"

Ironic, don't you think?

It was only when I was running through the crowd toward the exit that it dawned on me. I had no idea what I was going to do with the purse. Give it to the security guard? Give it to Hammy to pay him back for the mess I'd made of things? Give it to my mother for Christmas?

I never had a chance to figure it out. I turned around and saw Shane with his big arms around both girls. He even gets to be the hero, I thought. It seemed so unfair.

The next thing I knew, someone screamed, "I got him!"

I recognized the voice, but I couldn't place it until my feet were knocked out from under me and I was flying through the air.

Cupcake Katie.

Chapter Seventeen

I immediately became a YouTube sensation. Three million hits and climbing. You gotta love cell phones.

It could have been worse. I did get the purse and, after a short tussle, managed to convince the police that it contained all the evidence they needed to convict the girls.

Yes, *girls* with an *s*. Brooke—not her real name—was in on it too. In fact, she was the so-called mastermind. When she realized the security guard was onto her, she needed to find a place to hide. And I, moron that I was, happily gave it to her. The Frank Lee Better costume was perfect. No one would recognize her while she and Kelsey kept on pickpocketing.

The security guy was able to arrest them right there, thanks to the quick thinking of Shane Coolen. (There's a phrase you don't hear very often.) It turns out he didn't have his big arms around Brooke and Kelsey to comfort them. He was "detaining" them, as they say in police shows.

"How did you know to do that?" I asked him later.

He rolled his eyes as if the answer were totally obvious. "Dan," he said, picking wax out of his ear with his baby finger. "You look too pathetic half-naked to do something like that in public—unless, of course, it's absolutely necessary. You clearly needed my help."

I thanked him—although I wasn't sure I should have.

Hammy even forgave me. He was disappointed in me at first, but then all the publicity hit. Everyone wanted to try one of his Hogg's Doggs. Luckily, Shane and I were able to talk him into ditching the fiber and adding a bit of flavor by then. Before long, he was making so much money he didn't care about the ripped cape anymore.

But the best news was that Shane had been right about another thing too. She wasn't a meatball or a chicken nugget, but I did run into a girl that day. And when I say "run into," I mean "run into."

Sushi Sue just might turn out to be the girl for me. I really did knock her off her feet. We're going to spend some of the money we earned at the Food Fantasia Fun Fair to go out for pizza next week.

Vicki Grant is the bestselling author of numerous books for juveniles and young adults, including *Pigboy*, another Dan Hogg story in the Orca Currents series. Vicki lives in Halifax, Nova Scotia. For more information, visit www.vickigrant.com.

Titles in the Series

orca currents